The New Luxury

How rising global consciousness
is killing the Old Luxury Business

Josef Reisz

Copyright © 2018 Josef Reisz

All rights reserved.

ISBN: 1986215369
ISBN-13: 978-1986215367

Introduction 6

Greed was never good 8

Money is a tool 10

Money in Old Luxury has gone bad 12

High Price, Low Quality 14

Manifesto for Business Owners and Managers in Luxury 16

Grave Misjudgements by Sales People 17

Spirituality will drastically change the face of Luxury 19

Luxury is obsolete(?) 20

Can Old Luxury brands adapt? 21

But a business has to make money 23

Luxury has to come back to its senses 25

Business deafens People 26

The competition system 27

Luxury and its Key Factors 30

Exclusivity 30

Craftsmanship 33

All items are made by hand. 33

Price 36

Customers 38

Luring customers into their brand universe by making them think they need external gratification and appreciation 41

Separation 42

Exclusivity 43

Scarcity 44

Retail Experience 45

Retail = Separation 46

Negative Side Effects 47

Luxury, a commodity? 47

Ego 49

Ego Brands 49

The Ego in the Customer 50

Ego will die 52

High Profit Margins 53

You buy because you want to show off 55

Brand Name 56

Exploitation 58

Leather 59

Diamonds 61

Gold 62

The Rules of New Luxury 63

Individual Craftsmen on the rise 63

Transparency, or bust! 64

Goodbye, separation 65

Adding to Humanity 66

Highest quality is the key principle of life 67

Oneness 68

Key Factors of New Luxury 69

Quality 70

Sustainability 70

No growth for shareholders 71

Heart Space 73

Old Luxury = Ego. New Luxury = Heart 73

The Heart is Conscious. Just let it. 74

Heart holds no place for ego 75

The heart decides what to buy 75

Marketing is always deceitful 75

Old Luxury dies an unconscious death 76

Living in Harmony 78

The future of Luxury is in the labs of tomorrow 79

New Luxury Business Model 83

    Transparency 83

    Design 84

    Accessibility 85

    Adding to Humanity 86

    Giving back 87

About the Author 88

Introduction

I am writing this book because I feel that Luxury needs to *die* first in order to be re-born again.

Having had several businesses in the luxury markets from the early age of 20 on, I know how the luxury market today works and how customers are manipulated into thinking that they are valued. The honest truth is: At many well-known luxury brands, the customer means nothing unless they buy.

This may seem like a rather negative opening for this book, but it is my honest, inner truth. I have stopped thinking about what other people think of me a long time ago. What's important to me is to speak my truth and to bring awareness.

Old Luxury, as I like to call it, which is the Status Quo of luxury at the moment, has been gotten bigger and bigger and it reminds me a bit of the dinosaurs, that walked the earth. And we all know what happened to the dinosaurs. They thought they were too big to fail (die) and what is happening right now with the global rise in consciousness is that old dinosaur business models are dying.

Luxury has become more and more a commodity nowadays. Large, Old Luxury brands have managed to be everywhere, in the tiniest city and in the largest outlet centres, driving massive revenue by luring people into their so called brand universe.

The truth is, luxury has become a greedy, massive industry, with a handful of large conglomerate players on top, eating up every small innovative brand out there. Hidden from the public eye, they conduct the luxury business on the principles of massive profit growth instead of meticulous craftsmanship by hand.

One may argue about this perception but having been on the scene long enough, the greed out there is blatant for anyone to see.

Greed was never good

As much as I used to love the movie Wall Street and the legendary statement by Gordon Gecko: *"Greed is good"*, it does not resonate with me anymore.

Greed is rooted in ego. Greed is based upon fear. Fear is never good.

Greed is the physical expression of a lack and limitation mindset. If you believe that there is only so much of *XYZ* in the world, you become greedy.

You want to have more than anybody else. You start to horde it (money, in that case).

Greed is attached to Old Luxury and every negative emotion that goes along with it. Separation has been a major tool to increase greed among the customers, employees, managers, CEOs, brand owners. Separation is the idea that everyone is on their own. That you are different from anyone else. That black is white. That East is West. In fact, everything and everybody in this Universe is interconnected. So the concept of separation and greed, jealousy, envy, unworthiness, and so on, is obsolete and outdated.

Just as the dinosaurs did not see their end coming, Old Luxury is on the verge of extinction, as are all the old economic business models that are based upon lack, limitation, greed, separation, scarcity.

The truth is that there is enough for everybody on this planet to live life the to the fullest of everyone's potential. Nothing is holding you back, but your mind. Think abundance, live in abundance. Think lack, limitation, separation, Old Luxury, and you'll get just that.

Greed in all its forms is a major driver for Old Luxury. Marketing has been telling customers that they need to have this to feel good, need to buy that to be appreciated. Every marketing stunt has been designed to separate the so called elite from the others: Private Events, By Invitation Only appointments, Concierge Services, High Price tags, and so on. All of these marketing tricks are a primal trigger for the subconscious mind: *"Oh, when I get an invitation to a private event, I must be someone important."*

Again, the truth is that you are enough within yourself. In your heart space, you are already enough. You do not need to buy luxury to impress anyone or to feel loved or whole. You are already enough.

There is a difference in consciousness with New Luxury, i.e. luxury business models built upon the new rules of consciousness. There will still be *luxury* items and experiences, but not because only a few can afford it, no. Because life is meant to be lived in total abundance. Every item made to the highest quality standards is considered abundance because it adds tremendous value to humanity. So if you buy luxury, that is great, because you deserve abundance.

If you, however, receive an invitation to a private event, remember the separation mode this brand is in.

Money is a tool

Money is nothing but a tool. It can be used to enlighten humanity and move it to the next level.

Or it can be used to create jealously and separation.

In Old Luxury, money plays the dominant part of the mere definition of luxury. *If it ain't expensive enough (and therefore purchasable by the majority), it is not luxury.*

So money is integrated deeply into the DNA of luxury. The question is: Is this a good tool or a bad tool?

Money is part of our society and our life today. It will vanish one day completely, but as of now, we deal with money and we should do it in a conscious way. Hording money is not the answer, nor is throwing around lavishly with money.

Money should be used to enrich and enlighten humanity. Many billionaires are philanthropists, trying to make this world a better place, because they have become aware, they have come to a level of consciousness, they understand money as a means to all good on this planet.

Yes, of course, they buy luxury, but they don't buy it because they feel empty or need external appreciation. *Maybe some still do ;)*

They buy luxury because they realise that life is offering the best quality of everything. If you can afford the best food, the best medical treatments, the best clothes, you buy it because you live in abundance. There is a difference in buying for quality and buying because you need to fill your emptiness with a logo or brand name.

Truly rich people do not show off. Why would they? They just know their worth.

Money in Old Luxury has gone bad
When we take a look at how the luxury industry is built, money (high prices) are an essential part of the marketing strategy.

Even though a famous bag or luggage may only cost $500 in manufacturing, the retail price will be set to $5,000, $50,000 or even $150,000.

Price is a fundamental principle to work with separation between people who can afford it and people who cannot.

This principle is going away very soon as more and more people live their life in abundance because of a shift towards consciousness. Being aware means that you know that life is abundant and there is and infinite source of everything you desire: money, health, wealth, spirituality, relationship, and so on.

Money as a separator will not withstand the rise in global consciousness. Money has been used to make people think in lack, limitation and scarcity, to put people into debt over and over again, to make the struggle to make ends meet, to keep them in the drama of the 3D Matrix hamster wheel.

The concept of money is already changing. The frequency of money is changing from low to high. Low frequency is attached with fear, greed, lack, limitation, scarcity, anxiety, worry. High frequency money is attached with love, abundance, infinity, limitlessness.

High Price, Low Quality

Sometimes, a luxury brand pretends to be luxury when in reality it is just a fashion brand:

- high price points with low entry level points to lure the mass in
- Manufacturing is outsourced to low wages countries
- Animals are killed for leather
- Mass production
- And overproduction going on sale

What happens when the only factor of your luxury brand is the high price point and everything else is screaming „low quality mass market"? Take a minute to think about it and about the brands who would fit into this category.

Luxury has become a place of greed. People are ready to buy Old Luxury only through brand awareness. If you put enough money into brand awareness, you can sell anything at any price. As long as people stay unconscious, they will not question the brand if the brand makes them feel good.

As soon as consciousness arises, you see through the marketing tricks, through the patterns, the principles of how subconsciously you are being lured into buying, buying, buying.

Some well-known *luxury* brands have gone away with inferior quality, made in low wages countries, by people who need the money or else they'd starve. This is a business model based purely on separation in all areas and cannot withstand a conscious customer.

Consciousness makes us realise the connections between everyone and everything, and we begin to see and understand the connection of a business: Where do they manufacture, how do they manufacture, who do they hire, what do they pay, do they exploit animals and the planet or is their business model based on consciousness?

Today's technology makes it easy for everyone to ask these questions and make a conscious purchase decision based in the heart space, not the ego mind space.

Manifesto for Business Owners and Managers in Luxury

This book is meant to be a manifesto for today's and future luxury business owners and managers. I look around me and see the same patterns over and over again. Luxury has been dominated by the love for money (and we know: This is the root of all evil).

Luxury Business Managers are chasing their commissions, trying to achieve the goals set by the conglomerate mothership, pushing new collections out every year, but they forget the fundamental shift in consciousness that is going on right now.

Consumers and customers *(I wonder if we can still call them like that in New Luxury…)* are more aware than ever before in history. Today's technology makes it possible for anyone to research a company and how it conducts its business.

The barriers of information have been removed with the advent of the internet. Every piece of information is out there, one just needs to be aware of it and know where to look for it.

A brand needs to be fully transparent to show their consciousness. Hiding is over. Hiding behind numbers, behind a construct of corporations, behind massive retail stores, behind shareholders. Hiding is over. Transparency is consciousness, and demanded by conscious consumers. They know what they want to know and they know how to get that information. If the brands wants that or not. The brand is not being asked for permission anymore.

Grave Misjudgements by Sales People

I personally experienced how the first questions in a sales persons mind is: *"Does he have enough money? Can I get a commission out of him?"*. It is always stunning to me how superficial sales people can get in assessing a potential customer. Nowadays, you cannot tell anymore if someone lives in abundance, riches and wealth. But still some sales people only consider the outside, not inside.

Walk into a luxury jeweller with jeans and a polo shirt and the sales people might suspect that you have no means to buy even their least expensive piece.

Dress up with a suit, cufflinks, pocket square, bow tie and they will show you all their high priced lines.

The mind is deceitful above all things

The ego plays a dirty game with us in Old Luxury. Everybody who is involved and unconscious gets drawn into this game of lack, limitation, separation, worry, chasing the money.

> *This is not a book to blame everyone in Old Luxury, not at all. It is a book to bring awareness, this first spark of consciousness, this first question of: „Oh, I didn't know that. What else is there to know?"*

Spirituality will drastically change the face of Luxury

As global consciousness arises and the collective is coming out of their *sleep* and into awakening, the face of luxury will dramatically change. As more and more people become aware of their own existence, of their ego, of how mankind has exploited this planet since the dawn of humanity, more people are shifting their consciousness from separation to oneness.

They understand that we are all one, we are all interconnected with everything in the universe. This new understanding will change the face of *any* business and *any* market globally in a very short period of time. This awakening cannot be stopped nor avoided.

This wave of consciousness is riding throughout every institution, every industry, every business and everyone on this planet, slowly and gradually but continuously nevertheless.

Resisting this change will cause major damages within and without, no matter if human being or corporation. This wave of consciousness is the ultimate disruptive.

Luxury is obsolete(?)

In 10-20 years, luxury as we know it will have become obsolete. In fact, it has already become obsolete as I write this book in March 2018.

The old principles of luxury and how to build and run a luxury business have become outdated a long time ago. Yet, many of the global luxury brands in their conglomerate structures are trying to survive as did the Dinosaurs on this planet a long time ago.

This *game* will go on for some time but eventually, global luxury brands and their conglomerates will have to undergo a radical change or they will make way for the peaceful awakening of the planet.

It is not a question of want anymore. Bill Gates once said that you cannot decide if you want the internet or not. It is here in our lives and it will only grow.

I say about consciousness: *"You cannot choose if humanity will awaken. It is already happening and it cannot be stopped. Everyone who resists this awakening will eventually die."*

Luxury, in its present form of Old Luxury, will die unless undergoing major changes in their business model and corporate structure.

New Luxury is on the rise at the same magnificent speed as global consciousness rises. Its speed is hyperspeed. New Luxury will arise with high consciousness and awareness about sustainability, quality, animal / human rights, humanity. These will be the crucial factors for New Luxury brands and new business models in general.

Can Old Luxury brands adapt?

It is very likely that some Old Luxury brands can adapt if they let go of the ego mind. This means, to let go of the old beliefs of growth for growth sakes, shareholder value, being available in every major city of the world, and so on.

When global luxury brands and conglomerates reach a state of consciousness where they let go of killing animals, paying their workers and artisans more than enough, source manufacturing back into their own DNA, and let go of the idea of having to be visible everywhere, then these brands have a great chance to turn into New Luxury.

However, I still have to see a proof of consciousness within global and well-known luxury brands to go that path.

Many have adopted a kind of sustainability, which seems to be a mere marketing stunt. In reality, as long as a business is driven by financial goals and growth, sustainability and consciousness has little to say.

Making these changes requires the owner of the brands to make the shift in consciousness first. If the owner or CEO or highest level manager does not make this shift, if there is no sign of consciousness, the business will not sustain. Even if there is consciousness but other decision makers block it, the business will not sustain.

Again, this is not a question of do or do not, want or want not. It is a fact that consciousness is rising globally to a degree and speed that has never before seen in history of mankind.

These are exciting times for every human being, every business owner, every luxury manager, every CEO, every New Luxury brand. Adapting is not the premise. Letting go of old patterns is crucial, without resistance to the New.

But a business has to make money
Yes, any business has to make money to grow and pay their employees. The question is: Is making money and growth the main goal / purpose?

If the only purpose of a business is to make money, then any business principle will work. Consciousness has no place in such businesses. Businesses that are built upon exploiting this earth, its people and animals, show no signs of consciousness at all. They are now merely trying to survive because they feel the rising global consciousness and they are afraid to loose market share. Which is funny, because market share is based in ego, again. *(Greed, remember?)*

A business in New Luxury (or New Economy) will make more than enough money, because this is a natural process if you act with consciousness and awareness. Life is abundant, business is abundant, if your mind is abundant. If you restrict your mind with thoughts of market share, shareholder value, profit margins, expansion, growth, then abundance is not present within you and your business model.

More and more employees who awaken will leave their jobs and companies because they cannot add any value to a business who is not conducted with consciousness. This will lead to many companies loosing its workforce, but the people who are leaving won't be left alone, no. They will find new and exciting ways to live abundant lives. They will know how to make money without being in a corporation system.

This may lead to the thought that if everyone is living and abundant life, who will be left doing all the work?

Let's think about this for a moment.

Luxury has to come back to its senses

Luxury started out as a very special service. Creating an extremely well crafted item, very limited in quantity because it took a lot of skills and time to create it. Only available for some people, who would be able to visit the workshop or store in that city.

Then, the Industrial Revolution has brought greed into our *awareness* and businesses had to have the purpose of financial growth and expansion.

But how could you grow craftsmanship, high quality and limited supply?

Well, over the course of the past 200 years, the answer is simply: *By pretending it would still be of high quality, in limited quantity and made only by the greatest of craftsmanship.*

As a business grows, it is impossible to keep the high level of quality in craftsmanship, material, low quantities, and yet still retain a remarkable profit growth each year. It simply is not possible, without the help of our little marketeer friends.

Business deafens People

Business objectives or goals are deafening people. They stop listening to their heart and act purely from their mind space. They think that the mind knows all the logical answers, when in truth, only the heart knows what is wrong or right.

So what happens when deaf people are the decision makers? They act purely from their mind space, ignoring their hearts because that is not what is important to the overall business objective.

If more people took time off to go within themselves and listened to their hearts, we'd have a massive shift and surge in quitting jobs. People who are conscious see through the game of rising profits, expansion and marketing. It is all part of the machinery, but adds little to no value to humanity. It only adds to ego.

People with consciousness open their hearts, eyes, ears, and all other senses known or unknown to them.

They will see right through anything that is unconscious, not righteous or against humanity and this planet.

It is no wonder than the vegan movement is rising these days. More and more people become aware of the fact that every animal has the same right to life than any human.

In 10 years, we'll be looking back at how we killed 60 billion animals per year and wonder why on earth we thought that was a good thing.

Every industry undergoes dramatic changes with a rising global consciousness: Energy, Food, Farming, Luxury, Automobile, and many others too.

This shift is unavoidable and it is out of the question that many old business models will not survive.

The competition system

The system we live in right now is built upon external gratification. In Kindergarten, we get stars, in school we get grades, at university we get our diploma, at a job we get a monthly pay check. Everything in this society has been designed to keep us in separation mode, and in competition mode.

We have to let go of these beliefs before we can shift to a new consciousness.

These society structures have helped the rise of Old Luxury, and it will make room for New Luxury. In fact, New Luxury won't have to do anything but just sit there and wait for more people to become conscious and turn their backs on Old Luxury businesses.

Competition mode shows itself in every aspect of Old Luxury. When a company goes public, this is competition mode. When a company is thinking about growth, market share, shareholder value, that is competition mode.

There is no competition in nature. Everything is in perfect harmony, every growing and moving forward. There is enough for everyone and every business here on this planet and there is no need for any competition.

This concept is installed in us in school, university, business schools, business books, workshops and so on. We are so intrigued by having more than anyone else that greed is the natural effect of competition mode.

Greed is obsolete in New Luxury, and every New Business Model with consciousness.

Books have to be re-written, teachers have to be re-tired, businesses have to go out of business, all in the name of consciousness.

Now, this sounds dramatic and it is. However, the shift that we are already undergoing is not a hit over the head or slap in the face. You either become aware, become conscious, awaken, or you don't. And if you don't, you will not even notice the changes. You simply one day just die.

Luxury and its Key Factors

There are several key factors that make a luxury brand today and we shall take a look at them:

Exclusivity

Items are only available to those who can afford it.

This is a great misconception of Old Luxury today. As we have seen a rise in consciousness already, more people live their lives in abundance. This makes the old concept of *„only few people can afford it"* obsolete, despite setting ridiculously high price tags.

Old Luxury concepts are already obsolete as you read this book, but still marketing wants to ride this dead horse. The idea of being able to afford something is based in lack, limitation and scarcity minds, which will vanish as consciousness rise.

In New Luxury, almost anybody will be able to afford it, but it is a conscious decision to purchase it, not a decision influenced by tricky psychology marketing.

A conscious mind will be happy to pay the value of an item that is hand-made with utmost craftsmanship, sustainable, manufactured without harming others, and with great consciousness and spirituality. There will be a huge market for New Luxury, but the market will be conducted from the heart space, not the mind space.

The markets will not see any large scaled corporations or conglomerates because this would be against a conscious mind. There will be enough for everyone out there, and there already is enough. If we would just let go of our old business model ideas, we'd see the brightness and abundance.

Private invitation launch parties for the elite.

A masterpiece of marketing, it triggers the primal instincts of the guests and their ego is in full-on mode.

Why would you go to a private event? Because you want to feel special. You think you are special. You want to be among special people (elitist thinking).

Everything can be traced back to either ego or separation mode. Private events are the top of the ego mountain. As long as people are stuck in their ego, these private events will be a huge success. Someone who is conscious will think:"Why would I separate myself from others?"

The feel of oneness and wholeness makes these special things obsolete. I've seen a lot of private events in my life, also private member clubs, and so on. This is all rooted in ego mind, yet there are still so many private events / clubs in this world that even conscious people will have to deal with it at least for this life time. ;)

Items are only available in limited quantities, at certain places / stores.

Over the course of the past 50 years, Old Luxury brands have been invading the mass market like locusts.

New (Flagship) stores are being opened almost every week.

Old Luxury brands are embracing eCommerce more and more, selling over the internet.

Limited Quantities? Uh Huh.

The truth is: With more expansion of business, the more supply you need to manufacture.

If you have one store in, say, London, then you'd only have to make sure that this store has enough stock. Now multiply that by 10 stores in UK, 50 stores in Europe, 100 stores worldwide. Stock supply has to go up naturally which makes it a bit challenging to uphold the image of limited Old Luxury items.

Craftsmanship

All items are made by hand.

Possible for small, family-owned brands, but rather impossible for global enterprises.

And if they claim to do so, one could come to the conclusion that the highest quality levels can never be achieved by adding more craftsmen and artisans to the equation.

Highest quality items have to be produced by highly skilled craftsmen. Yes, you can increase the brand's output by hiring 50 more highly skilled craftsmen, but you also have to train them, maybe even for a year or two.

Although this might be possible, the sheer number of items that need to be produced can make you question that.

Craftsmanship in its purity is creating a special item by hand. Now, there will be conscious industries without much handmade craftsmanship. That's alright. But when we speak about New Luxury, we notice that the old principles and values will see a tremendous comeback. Handmade. Meticulousness. Limited. Conscious Creations. This really is something to embrace because this is true abundance.

No machine is included in the process of manufacturing.

What is meant are industrialised processes as we have seen with the advent of the Industrial Revolution.

Some machines will be used even in small New Luxury brands.

But no machinery in general means that there is no way to mass produce for a global business.

Using machines enables a company to scale its business dramatically, producing thousands and hundreds of thousands of identical looking items for their hundreds of stores worldwide, incl their online store.

Only a few people / families still know the secrets of such a craftsmanship, trying to uphold it in modern times.

Even though, some conglomerates try to buy more and more off these small brands just to get their skills. It is highly debatable if this is a sustainable business model.

For New Luxury, we will see that conglomerates have no future since their only goal is to increase their profits and revenues. In New Luxury, people are very aware of these constructs and will see through these principles.

Being conscious means to support the local craftsman because you can identify with them. You do not need to wear a brand logo. You become aware that wearing something from a local craftsman, without any branding, is much more sustainable and conscious.

There will be no need for labels anymore. The need will be for utmost quality. And if there is someone in your city or country who creates the finest widgets of XYZ, you are most likely to buy from them when trust has been built up.

Price

High price tags that is meant to make the customers think of higher quality.

Let us consciously think about how it is possible to ask $100 for a polo shirt or t-shirt that is manufactured in the same workshops as a shirt for $10-20.

The quality of these items do not differ much, if they do at all.

Yes, there might be some exceptions to the rule where a high price tag does indeed equal highest quality standards. However, one can come to the conclusion that these items then cannot be produced for the mass of retail stores an Old Luxury brand might entertain.

High prices to separate those who cannot afford it from those who easily can.

Separation is everywhere in Old Luxury and high prices are a *great* tool to make people think that they are superior to others, or inferior if they cannot afford this or that item.

Desires plays a great role in the marketing of Old Luxury, however, these desires are rooted in ego and will dissolve with the rise of global consciousness.

Old Luxury cannot convince a conscious person that he or she *needs* this item. If there is a desire for a high quality item in that person, he or she will do their research according to the Rules of New Luxury.

With a conscious mind, there cannot be separation from anyone, and businesses need to understand that if they continue their journey with separation practices, they will go downhills very soon. Separation worked for Old Luxury but it will not work for New Luxury.

Unity and Oneness will be the New Luxury credo and it will be an exciting journey to see how this comes to life.

Customers

Only few people can afford the high prices, thus making it exclusive. However, with rising consciousness, more people live their lives in abundance, hence, more people are able to buy high priced items.

So luxury will not be able to convince someone with a conscious mind. No matter how exclusive an item is. If the brand lack consciousness in its business model, it simply does not resonate with conscious customers.

This is the main difference in how New Luxury conducts business. Moving away from separation and ego, towards unity, oneness and harmony.

Making customers feel special because they wear or buy this or that brand

Brand Awareness will be turn inside out in New Luxury. A brand does not need to be shown off by someone who buys an item. Brands or logos and labels will become obsolete because consciousness does not need to show off.

It is enough for someone to buy the highest quality without the need for showing off a brand name. In fact, customers will become so aware as to demand the removal of any logo from the items that they buy.

Highest quality is something that comes from within, not without. It is enough for a conscious person to know that they wear a polo shirt of the highest material quality, with utmost awareness to the environment and the manufacturing process.

Yes, a brand name will still be important to spread the word. And the brand owners must do their utmost with great consciousness to build new strategies and marketing plans. (Actually, marketing might become obsolete to a degree too). A brand wants to be known, which in itself is ego, but necessary to spread the word, of course. If done in a very conscious way, the right customers will be attracted effortlessly and without or little marketing budget.

Old Luxury brands are throwing millions and billions into the accounts of social media, advertising, magazines, brand awareness, and so on. This is pushing and resisting the change. They are pushing their messages outside, hoping that it will resonate with someone.

Marketing in New Luxury will have to re-think their ways because everything they were taught in marketing schools, have become obsolete.

New ways have to be defined, new goals, new ways of communication. It needs great minds to make that shift for the whole industry, but these minds are already out there, waiting for their awakening. Or they have already awakened and are moving on their path to a conscious business model.

Luring customers into their brand universe by making them think they need external gratification and appreciation

This Old Luxury principle has already begun to break apart. With rising awareness within people, there is no need to feel external gratification. In fact, consciousness shows us that we are whole. We are one within. We are enough.

No Old Luxury marketeer will be able to break through a conscious person's heart space with tempting, subconscious messaging.

Customers will become very aware and conscious about the marketing tricks and they will question every little detail about a New Luxury item.

And a brand had better prepared for this now before it might be too late.

Separation

Luxury today is based on the principle of separation. Everything in the marketing and brand strategy of worldwide, big luxury brands have the stench of separation.

They say that only a few people can afford their items, when in reality, the huge luxury conglomerates are only acting for shareholder value (when they have gone public). Adding shareholder value first means that you must grow your business every year, no matter what. You must find new customers, create new lines of products, expand in new territories. Hence, separation is an idea that is still being held up by Old Luxury marketing. But in fact, Old Luxury has become a commodity and a lot of people can afford it. People who still think they need this external gratification by wearing and showing off a certain brand or label.

So after all, this exclusivity that is proposed by the luxury brands themselves in their marketing is nothing but a hoax to lure people into their brand universe.

Exclusivity

Luxury items are very exclusive items, only available for the *chosen few*, we are told to believe. Everything is pointing in this direction. The creators do not want everyone to have, wear or buy their items, only those who can afford it. Hence, the high price tag.

But as explained, there is no real exclusivity anymore in today's times. Global, well-known luxury brands have a turnover of multi-billion dollars. There is no place anymore for exclusivity because you simply would not get the turnover you need, which is unsustainable for a business of that size.

The only way to return to true exclusivity and natural scarcity is to make a conscious decision away from growth and towards a smaller sized business that is sustainable and profitable. Cutting down half of the retail stores? Maybe, why not? Everything that has to go, will go, to get to consciousness.

Scarcity

With great craftsmanship comes a natural scarcity of the items. It takes time and great skills to produce an item and so there occurs a natural limitation.

While this natural appearance of scarcity is not necessarily a bad thing, global luxury brands have mastered the craft of artificial scarcity. This means that the limitation is not due to the time involved in creating it, but due to marketing reasons.

Scarcity is not scarcity anymore, it is an artificial construct, invented to trigger our ego driven purchase decision right on the spot. With scarcity in place, a brand can put a higher price tag on the item, proclaiming its exclusivity, when in reality, the brand has the ability to mass produce this item.

But for the sake of separation, scarcity has to be put in place because in order for separation to work, you need people who are willing to pay a high price and people who desperately want to be able to afford such an item. Separation creates jealously creates anger creates hate.

Retail Experience

The retail experience of any global, well-known luxury brand is to impress the person who enters the *realms*.

Also, it is to intimidate everyone before their purchase. The customer is to be WOWed so he or she stands in awe of the brand's products. But the truth is, Old Luxury retail stores are almost designed to be a temple or church for the brand. That is done on purpose because religion has been working with sin, blame and guilt for thousands of years.

So what happens when you enter and Old Luxury Church? You feel unworthy, you feel you have sinned, you feel you must fill the void in your heart with all the goodies that the *pastors* are offering you in this sacred realm.

A bold theory? Maybe. If I am wrong, I am wrong. But I wasn't in doubt when writing it. ;)

Retail = Separation

This is achieved by combining the brand's pieces with art, interior design, sales personnel, a certain atmosphere, guards at the doorsteps, and so on.

This, too, is a form of separation, to separate those who can and will afford it from those who feel the desire arising to „one day" being able to buy at least a cheaper item of this or that brand.

It is separation in its highest form, disguised by the sense of luxury.

Luxury is the greatest separator in our world today. People who can easily afford it and people who can hardly dream about. People who love to show what they can afford, and people who buy only what they think they can afford.

If you have ever walked down New Bond Street in London, you see that most jewellers have bodyguards at their front door. Yes, they say it is because they don't want to run the risk of being robbed, which might be true. But just keep separation in mind and there is another picture unfolding.

Negative Side Effects

This separation is a dangerous tool for humanity and the luxury sector because it brings negative side effects with it: envy, jealously, the feeling of not being worthy, the feeling of not deserving, the feeling of „I Have to buy this to show others who I am".

All these emotions that human beings attach to luxury are a separator. Since the New Luxury understands in its consciousness that we are all connected, we are one, there is no need for separation because everybody can have total abundance, riches and wealth.

Luxury, a commodity?

So what happens to luxury if everybody can afford it? It simply becomes a commodity.

That is why Old Luxury marketers are constantly trying to trigger the customers' ego and primal instincts either by artificial scarcity, polarity, provocation, tasteless designs, or some other marketing stunt.

People who are conscious cannot be triggered like that. Old Luxury knows that is scarred to death of it.

Ego

Ego Brands

The whole luxury market is rooted in the egoic mind. Both, the global luxury brands today in their pursuit of shareholder value, as well as the luxury customers today, have a strong egoic state of mind when it comes to showing off their luxury.

Brands are caught up in their pursuit of adding more and more value to the shareholders through ridiculous growth every year and tremendous profit margins.

They have lost their own roots of how they started: With just one person in their workshops 200 years ago, creating the magic for very few customers.

When we go back to these days, we see that the creator has little ego in mind when creating their items. The pure joy of creating a masterpiece is an almost spiritual experience that requires full presence and consciousness.

So the history of Old Luxury began in the heart space but ended up in mind space, where ego mind has completely taken over the once truly inspirational values and principles.

Creating a piece of high luxury is a spiritual, meditative experience for the creator if he or she takes their time to create it. If time is a measurable component in the profit margin, the spiritual experience of creating something magnificence turns into stress and anxiety.

The Ego in the Customer

Most luxury customers have the installed belief that they have to buy luxury brand names to feel better. Buying luxury to show off the brand name is ego in its purest form. These customers are trying to fill a void in their being. And they think that a luxury item will fill it. They think that somebody else will fill it, even. They fail to realise in their unconsciousness that it is only they themselves who can fill the whole in their heart space. No luxury item can do that for them.

Ego is luring us into believing that our self-worth can only be measured by external things: luxury items, words of appreciation, school grades, the jealousy of others, awards, etc. The truth is that our self-worth is always within us, never on the outside.

Our self-worth lives inside our heart space, but society has taught us to listen to our mind and not our heart. And this is where the ego can unfold its true power. Ego resides within the mind. All these thoughts of worry, fear, lack, limitation, no self-worth, etc, originate in our egoic mind.

And the external expression of an ego mind with little self-worth are the items one has to buy to feel worthy. In your heart, you are enough. Your heart has told you all along that you do not need to buy things to feel good or impress others. You can enjoy luxury items but only if you are not attached to them.

And with rising awareness, this detachment from things happens automatically.

Ego will die

At some point in time, ego will die and therefore a large reason for buying luxury. The Rules of New Luxury clearly say that ego has no say in what customers purchase once they have experienced their awakening and are in their conscious state of mind.

Showing off brand names is a game of the past. And as the global ego continues to die, so does the need to show off, to impress others, or fill the whole with something external.

We know that we are enough. We know that the Wholeness is within us. We just have to let go of everything that does not serve our heart space. If we loose our attachments to things, items and even people, we realise that we are whole, we are enough and we are unconditional love.

Buying Old Luxury shows a lack of unconditional love because the decision is made by the mind, not the heart that: „I need to have this now".

Once consciousness arises, the heart becomes the decision maker again. Customers become more aware of the fact that we are all interconnected. They will question old business models (in all sectors) and move towards those companies with a conscious business model.

High Profit Margins

Now, at the time when Old Luxury emerged (100-200 years ago), high profit margins were perfectly fine because the craftsman could not have possibly created 1,000 items per month. It was rather 1 - 10 pieces per month. Hence, a high profit margin was necessary for the creator's survival.

Still today, small luxury companies need to have their high profit margins, not because they act from artificial scarcity or separation, no. They have to have these profit margins in order to keep the business running without the need of outside investors or compromising on quality.

Making money does not contradict consciousness. Living consciously and aware means to live in full abundance, wealth and riches. So it is everybody's birth right to enjoy everything in this lifetime. Money is a part of our society today and until it will have become obsolete, it is our right to have more than enough money to fulfil our desires, wishes, dreams and still have more than enough to do good and follow our purpose.

There is no lack of money, however Old Luxury and Old Economy has installed this scarcity belief in us that there is not enough money available for everyone. That is clearly not true since money is just an idea. It is created out of thin air and it will vanish into thin air again one day.

Until then, making money is a wonderful way of experiencing life to the fullest of its splendour when it is used in an enlightening, righteous, enriching way.

You buy because you want to show off

Most luxury purchasers are buying a specific brand to show that they can afford that brand. This reason is totally rooted in an egoic mind.

If you'd act from your heart space, you would not care about any brand name. You would care about the rules of the New Luxury, no matter the brand name.

Brand names are a very important factor in today's Old Luxury market because they had been build up for 100-200 years and have a strong recognisability and value for the company or conglomerate.

Unfortunately, there are many luxury customers out in the world who are not aware and not conscious enough to tell the brands what they really want. Once you have become aware and conscious of the Rules of New Luxury (part 2 of this book), you immediately realise the madness on how a global, well-known luxury brand exploits its own heritage and the planet today.

Instagram - The Centre of Ego

Instagram has become the centre of ego nowadays, it seems. People are sharing themselves (selfies) for external gratifications (likes, comments). This is the summit of ego but it has been so well designed that we do not even realise it. Being conscious means, being immune against any outside gratification because you know that you are enough and you are radiating unconditional love.

Instagram and other social media platforms have managed to get people even more into their egoic mind, away from their heart space. For marketers and brands, this is hilariously great because ego sells.

Forget about „sex sells". It is „ego sells" today in Old Luxury.

Brand Name

Global, well-known luxury brands are riding their dead horse (brand) that has been established for 100-

200 years now, adding no value to humanity. Or in simple terms: Without their name, they'd be dead.

Brand names will be completely obsolete as a driving force behind a purchase in New Luxury. Simply because the brand name is less important than the consciousness and awareness of the brand itself.

If the brand owner is conscious about the interconnectedness of everything in the universe, it will reflect on the brand's portfolio, its communication and manufacturing process.

Yes, Brands will still be around because although consciousness rises, the brand still needs to present itself and be open for its customers or potential new conscious customers.

But the main difference will be that brands will be asked to remove their labels and logos from their items, because the customers do not buy for a brand or logo anymore. They buy because they made a conscious decision.

Exploitation

The Luxury market exploits nature and animals for the sake of high price tags.

At our own family-owned luxury and fine jewelry company UDOZZO, we have decided against launching a leather collection of small leather items because we did not want to participate in exploiting animals or nature as other global, well-known brands have been doing.

Personally, I have seen all the exotic leather out there: snake, alligator, crocodile, stingray, python, but also regular leather from horses, cows and so on. It is a pure exploitation of the natural connectedness. We are all connected with everything in the Universe, but still we think we have more right to live than any other of these animals? Why is that so? Why would anyone need to wear leather, exotic leather and pay a ridiculous high price for it just because there is a well-known brand name on it which we have been taught to trust?

All markets today are exploiting animals, human beings, and the planet itself by sourcing their materials for the mass markets. It is madness to think that we can slaughter an estimated 60 billion animals each year without having to pay the price for it.

Leather

Most global, well-known luxury brands have leather collections. Some of them also carry exotic leather. These animals are killed for the pure ego state of mind of the owners of the luxury brand as well as the brand's customers. As long as these brands keep producing leather collections *(in some cases, their whole business and brand is based upon being the „masters of leather")* and as long as their customers keep buying these leather products, we can establish that there is zero consciousness and awareness.

There needs to be a shift to consciousness before the killing of animals will stop completely, but I have the strongest confidence within me that we will see this drastic shift within our lifetime.

Lab Grown Leather is the future

Yes, it will take some time to have lab grown leather or faux leather without the environmental affects that it still has today, but the shift is inevitable.

True leather or exotic leather is already loosing its lustre for people who are conscious and awake. Sometimes, it is still inevitable to avoid leather, yes, but the global consciousness will bring new and better solutions for the issues that we have today.

More and more Old Luxury brands are ditching the idea of leather or fur already, if for the right reasons we do not know. At least, there seems to be a spark of consciousness. Everything that contributes to the global shift in consciousness needs to be embraced, no matter where it comes from.

Diamonds

Another great material for luxury brands are diamonds. These precious gemstones are brought up from Mother Earth with great effort and negative effects on the environment and the people working to find diamonds and gemstones.

Diamonds have always been fascinating for people because of their scarcity and colour. Well, actually, to be quite honest with you, diamonds are not as scarce as you might think.

There was a global marketing campaign initiated in the early 20th century that encouraged men to buy diamond rings for their engagement and proposal to their women. This newly created tradition was so successful that it started the diamond market as we know today.

The negative effects on the environment and people of how diamonds are mined today cannot sustain in a world of global consciousness.

Gold

As for our family-owned group of companies, Von Urbanovsky, we have decided to only source our gold from sustainable sources. And we found these sources (families or individual miners who run their own small gold mining businesses) in no other country than Finland.

The country has tremendous laws in place that protects nature and the environment. Sourcing from our partners in Finland, we can make sure that we avoid the global diamond markets dominated by a few players who make the rules.

Being a family business, working with families and individuals has always been our primary goal in everything we do and how we conduct our business.

Traditionally, gold has dramatic effects on the environment and the people mining gold. Hence, it cannot sustain in New Luxury and new methods and/or materials will have to be used and invented.

The Rules of New Luxury

Now that we have taken a look at the rules of Old Luxury, it is time to think about New Luxury. As consciousness awakens in more and more people on this planet, we as humanity will rise above the egoic mind, external factors to fill in the holes in our heart, separation mode, competition mode, and so on.

All these factors that were there to define luxury in the old days are gone because awareness makes them obsolete.

Individual Craftsmen on the rise

I predict that we will see the rise of small, family owned workshops around the world, each perfect in their craftsmanship, producing high quality items in a sustainable manner and naturally limited supply.

They will not turn into a global corporation because they value what they do locally. Customers who are interested will have to come to the workshop or buy online. eCommerce will play a great role for New Luxury to make sales and communicate with customers.

New Luxury companies will be family-owned, with a small number of highly conscious and passionate employees, highly skilled craftsmen, and a purpose.

This purpose is the driving force behind every decision. These smaller companies utilise modern technology at its best without luring customers into thinking, but rather presenting themselves and attracting the right customers.

Transparency, or bust!
The days of mass luxury, as conducted by the global, well-known brands and conglomerates today, are gone. Customers will not be lured into a brand by triggering their egoic mind, no. Customers will become more and more savvy about the sustainability of

a brand, about the manufacturing process and the materials used.

In fact, it will be part of the brands DNA to be as transparent as possible. If a customers wants to talk to the CEO, there will be a way.

Customers will want to know about the materials used, where its sourced, how an item is manufactured, where, and what else is involved.

Price will not play a role because the value that is added weighs more than the price. As consciousness rises, more people will live abundant lives where money is not an issue anymore.

Goodbye, separation

Luxury has always been conducted in the very way of separating the *good* from the *bad*. Luxury CEOs have been in their ivory towers, playing their luxury game on the backs of people who need to earn the money in low wages countries, and the backs of animals, and the backs of their customers.

Keeping customers in the dark will not sustain in New Luxury. Transparency is Key.

Separation had its part but is now out of the game. Oneness is key in New Luxury.

Adding to Humanity

As global consciousness arises, any business must align with the principles of awareness and consciousness. If a business is not conducted with awareness and consciousness, i.e. in separation mode, competition mode, then this business is bound to go out of business very soon.

New Luxury adds to humanity by simply remaining true to two fundamental key principles:

– Highest Quality

– Sustainability

These two factors will define not only New Luxury but also any business on this planet as more and more people become aware.

Highest quality is the key principle of life

Life itself does not settle down for anything less than highest quality. Low quality does not survive because everything in the universe and on this planet is in perfect, high frequency harmony.

Mankind, however, has managed to be the low frequency in this world, messing up the natural harmony by implementing a system of separation, anxiety, worry, lack, limitation and fear.

This will not sustain in New Luxury because being aware means to understand the natural harmony of everything. We are interconnected with everything and everyone, hence there is no need for any low quality items or anything that is unsustainable.

Oneness

As awareness and consciousness arises on the planet, people understand more and more than society has planted in us the seed of separation to keep us in the hamster wheel (or 3D Matrix, if you like to goole ;).

Separation is a war monger, a bringer and sustainer of poverty, jealousy, envy, ego, low self-esteem, external satisfaction factors, and so on.

The simple idea of separation can be seen in the borders of the countries, racism, hate, jealously. None of these things can survive with a conscious person, because a person who is aware knows that nothing in this Universe is separated. We are all one. Everything is interconnected. You are connected to the animal skin you wear, as well as the child labor manufacturing of your fashion.

When we rise our consciousness, we understand that everything and everybody comes from the same source and we are all connected. We understand the absurdity of separation in our every-day-life.

Every human being and every animal has the same right to live, there is no separation in superior life form and inferior life form.

We will move towards a society where brands act for the good of humanity and not shareholders. In fact, shareholders are obsolete because their first and foremost goal is to increase their profit.

In a world where most people live conscious lives, we understand the madness of money that we were taught to belief. And we also understand that everybody will live in abundance, wealth and riches to the extend as he or she is capable of receiving it. Money is a state of mind, and hence we must conclude that so is luxury.

Key Factors of New Luxury

We have taken a look at some key factors of old luxury. Now we must understand the factors for New Luxury in a world of conscious customers.

Quality

Still, quality will remain the key factor because once you live an abundant life, why would you settle for low quality? Highest quality is your birth right and hence you should only buy highest quality.

Quality remains one of the two main factors for New Luxury because it is aligned with consciousness. Everything in life is of highest quality, adding to the greater good of humanity.

Everything that does not contribute to the highest quality of life and humanity will not survive. Not in New Luxury, or New Economy, or New Earth.

Sustainability

Sustainability starting from the materials, the environment, the people in the workshops is the only true factor that remains in New Luxury.

If a brand is not willing to adapt to an utmost sustainable business model, it will become obsolete.

Sustainability in all areas means to have control over the whole manufacturing process, not outsourcing anything, in-house-production only, natural scarcity due to the limitation of qualified craftsmen and artisans.

What we can conclude from that is that the big, global luxury brands and conglomerates that we have today are a thing of the past. They will be torn apart in a peaceful way by the rising global, collective consciousness.

No growth for shareholders

Growth for Growth sakes is not a factor in New Luxury anymore. Growth in a spiritual meaning, is, though!. Spiritual growth will be part of any business as awareness rises on this planet. It is inevitable and we should embrace it.

Shareholders will have a hard time, especially in New Luxury, simply because there will be no more shares out there to hold.

The New Luxury is comprised of small, family-owned businesses who have dedicated to sustainability, highest quality, honesty, transparency and natural growth. Yes, their business will grow over time, but there is no need to grow into a multi-billion dollar corporation or merge into conglomerates.

Heart Space

The opposite of our ego mind is our heart space. In fact, our heart is the master over our mind. However, mind has tricked us into thinking that mind is the master. But you see, the heart, knowing that it is the true master, does not have to prove anything and let's mind play its childish games until we become aware and conscious. Then, our heart will take over control again and our mind remains as our servant, as a tool, only.

Old Luxury = Ego. New Luxury = Heart
Old Luxury has been feeding the egos of so many unaware customers. The brand, or rather the minds behind the brands, lured customers into thinking that buying a specific brand or item will make the customer feel happy, worthy, whole.

This is separation mode par excellence.

In heart space, there is no place for ego. Being in heart space, customers do not buy in order to fill the void in their heart, because there is no void to fill. People are conscious enough to feel their own worth from within, not from any outside item or appreciation.

Heart space is the only space where we *feel* what to buy. Our heart helps us to dig through the subconscious marketing messages so cleverly designed that our minds command us to buy things we don't need, can't afford or simply are crap.

The Heart is Conscious. Just let it.
Listening to your heart means listening to your own inner truth. Your mind does not tell you the truth. Mind is always thinking, thinking, thinking. Mind is fearful, always.

Your heart can tell you what to do if only you let it. Your heart has a very strong voice but the distractions of our days make us ignore this voice. It is, after all, the only true voice we have that comes from our heart and soul. It is madness to think with our minds rather than to listen to our hearts.

Heart holds no place for ego

As global consciousness rises, more and more people get or are born into their heart space. This space where we listen to our feelings, our intuition, our emotions, is the only place from where we should make life changing decisions.

The mind is a great tool with which we can look into the details if necessary. But our heart tells us where our life is going.

The heart decides what to buy

Once we have come back home into our heart space, marketing will not be able to influence our purchase decision anymore.

Marketing is always deceitful

Let us understand what marketing is, actually.

Marketing is trying to tell you what to buy, when to buy it, from whom to buy it and whom to show it. Marketing is a very deceitful tool of Old Luxury and Old Economy because unconscious people are receptive for *anything*.

When you are not aware and unconscious, everything your hear, read or talk about is on the subconscious level. And marketing is targeting and triggering your primal, subconscious mind with all kinds of luring messages. *Buy this to feel better. Buy that to feel superior.* For someone who is conscious enough to see through this tool of mass manipulation, nothing of it makes sense. None of these messages can even get to their mind because the heart space is building up a protection shield against unconscious messages and people.

Old Luxury dies an unconscious death
As time goes by, people who are not aware, who do not get to their heart space, who cannot reach a level of consciousness, will die.

It is happening already. People who are unconscious of their health are dying of cancer. It is a natural process that goes along with (un)consciousness. The longer you stay unconscious, the earlier you start to die on the inside.

Getting into your heart space will lift the frequencies of your vibrations and hence making you immune against mass manipulation from Old Luxury brand marketing.

Once you become aware, your purchasing decisions will drastically change. You will change the way you buy, what you buy, from whom you buy, what you wear, what your consume, what you eat.

Living in Harmony

One major aspect of Old Luxury, and basically any business today, is the exploitation of animals, people and nature.

There is little to no awareness in large corporations today about how to add to humanity, how everything is connected, how everything is one. Still, corporations today exist to make profit and money.

However, as consciousness rises globally, we become more and more aware of the fact that money may be still a factor for the next generations, but making money is never the goal.

Adding value to humanity, to the environment, to Earth and the animal kingdom is the only way of how a business will thrive within the next 10-20 years. In Luxury and other industry sectors.

New Luxury understands that we are all interconnected. We are one with the animals that are slaughtered for food or their skin. We are one with the low wage worker dying the jeans or polo shirts we wear.

We become more and more aware of the Oneness of everything and our heart space is telling us to let go of separation and start living a life in perfect harmony with everything and everyone.

The future of Luxury is in the labs of tomorrow

Luxury is the melting pot of craftsmanship, art, skills, rare materials, scarcity, heritage, history, myth. In recent years, the luxury market got bloated with growth, driving luxury Maisons into thinking that „more is more".

But from a luxury brand's point of view, this is highly dangerous. The paradigm of luxury has always been that the more scarce it is, the more desirable it becomes. And the more available it is, the less desirable luxury becomes.

Having an eye on sustainability, the above-mentioned key factors of luxury have to undergo a massive change. In particular, it is the „rare material" that will dramatically change the face of luxury. Nowadays, the epitome of luxury material is diamonds, gold, leather and when one takes a look at how these materials are sourced, one can hardly speak about sustainability.

What can be lab grown will be lab grown

It will take at least 5 more generations until mankind is able to live in perfect harmony with its environment. A long way to go but it is necessary to start now and take small steps towards true sustainability.

It is inevitable for mankind and luxury that it moves away from natural resources like diamonds, gold and leather. One can argue back and fourth about how sustainably these materials are being sourced today. The fact is that as long as other creatures, countries and societies are made to suffer by the desire of a few, we are far away from sustainability.

Leather, as a natural resource for our humanly pleasures, will vanish within the next two generations completely. So will natural diamonds. Everything will come from the labs, and if you are scared of this future, you're about to get extinct by Mother Nature.

As inevitable as the internet and technology is, so is the transformation from natural resources to artificial resources.

Luxury will change its face and its core.

It will embrace lab grown diamonds, gold and leather because this is the only true sustainable way when we want to cut out any suffering, suppression and greed from the supply chain.

The lab grown materials will certainly be cheaper than the natural resources. And hence, more people might be able to afford diamonds then. But then, luxury has to re-invent itself from the core.

The questions will then have to be:

- What are the factors that make luxury?

- Once luxury has gone beyond rare material and unique design, what is its USP?

Since extraordinary design has been taken to the mass market, luxury's focus on superior craftsmanship for limited quantities will make a huge comeback. It matters less what materials are being used, after the natural resource leather will have vanished from the mass market. What will prevail though is the essence of pure craftsmanship.

Luxury has to re-invent itself and become the pioneers and visionaries that they had been 200 years ago in order to maintain their position as a valid player in today's world.

New Luxury Business Model

There will be a few principles upon which we can build a New Luxury business model:

Transparency

Total transparency is a prerequisite nowadays. Rising consciousness makes customers more aware of how a company conducts business.

If the customer has a question, it is expected to be answered with utmost honesty and integrity.

If the company has something to hide in their manufacturing process or marketing, it will soon become very obvious.

So base your New Luxury business upon unshakable principles that are in line with the Rules of New Luxury.

Design

As great design has become a commodity, the design itself will become more and more important.

For a small, family-owned New Luxury brand, it can be enough to focus on only one item. Yes, it can be enough to create an amazing item according to the Rules of New Luxury.

More items could be considered a distraction from the brand's core values.

The design has to resonate with the new, rising consciousness, too. The days of cheesy designs that have absolutely no story behind it, are over.

The conscious consumer demands something meaningful. He or she wants to know the story behind a product, why it was created in the first place and what it makes so special.

It can be a bespoke item, made to the customer, who holds a very special bond with a certain design.

Or it can be a design that touches them deeply in their spirituality, consciousness, personal growth.

Accessibility

Old Luxury lives in separation mode and hence it is very hard to reach out to the people responsible for a brand.

The New Luxury demands the owner of the businesses to be accessible to questions or interviews.

Small, family-owned companies are already great a customer service because to them, every customer is valued, and they know every customer by heart.

This is the new marketing, the new customer retention, the new customer service.

If you have 250,000 entries in your customer database, that is exactly how you treat it: as entries.

If you have 100 people in your customer list, you know every single one by heart, their likes and dislikes, birthdays, pets, children, spouse, etc and so on.

Customer service is really turning into relationship. A relationship based upon the knowledge that we are all one, interconnected and not separate from each other.

Adding to Humanity

A brand will not survive in New Luxury if it doesn't contribute to humanity. If a brand just keeps hording their profits, the brand will die. If a brand uses its money to exploit people and keep them in poverty, the brand will die.

Consciousness brings with it a great freedom: Do the right thing.

And *right* is not defined by some ego society ideas of what right is. Right is the universal language of your heart space. You know instantly if something is right or wrong. You do not have to think about it.

This applies for both, the brand and the customer. The brand owners know immediately what to do and where to go to add to humanity in a righteous way. And the conscious customers will be drawn to the right brand that resonates with them.

A company that is built on lies, supports unethical practices, kills animals, exploits nature and people will experience a drastic decline in business as global consciousness arises, and eventually will go out of business.

Giving back

Along with adding to humanity, giving back is a fundamental principle of a conscious business. I do not mean meaningless charity events that are again rooted in ego. Every business in New Luxury will have their own purpose, which derives from the owners personal purpose. It can be to support a new education system, or to support world health, or an animal or environment project. Whatever it is, it has to be very transparent. The customers will want to know that the brand is doing good with the money and not only hording it for shareholder value sakes.

A purpose is the driving force behind everyone and a brand has the opportunity and responsibility to do everything it can to contribute, add value and support the evolution of humanity.

About the Author

Josef Reisz is the creator of RICH RELATIONSHIP, a method that can lift your relationship to the next level in awareness, growth and spirituality.

Having started half a dozen companies, he is now CEO of Von Urbanovsky (a group of High Luxury companies), UDOZZO - Fine Jewelry and PRAGMA (a high level matchmaking agency)

Von Urbanovsky is the name of his great-grandmother, providing the brand with the family values and seriousness necessary in today's business world.

www.VonUrbanovsky.com
www.Udozzo.com
www.Pragma.love

FOLLOW JOSEF

Instagram http://www.instagram.comjosefreisz
Twitter http://www.twitter.com/josefreisz
LinkedIn https://www.linkedin.com/in/josefreisz

Printed in Poland
by Amazon Fulfillment
Poland Sp. z o.o., Wrocław